Translation,
the bass accompaniment

Other works by Deborah Meadows include:

Saccade Patterns (BlazeVOX, 2011)
How, the means (Mindmade Books, 2010)
Depleted Burden Down (Factory School, 2009)
Goodbye Tissues (Shearsman Books, 2009)
involutia (Shearsman Books, 2007)
The Draped Universe (Belladonna* Books, 2007)
Thin Gloves (Green Integer, 2006)
Growing Still (Tinfish Press, 2005)
Itinerant Men (Krupskaya Press, 2004)
Representing Absence (Green Integer, 2004)
"*The 60's and 70's:* from *The Theory of Subjectivity in* Moby-Dick"
                (Tinfish Press, 2003)

Deborah Meadows

Translation,
the bass accompaniment

—*Selected Poems*—

Shearsman Books

First published in the United Kingdom in 2013 by
Shearsman Books Ltd
50 Westons Hill Drive
Emersons Green
BRISTOL
BS16 7DF

Shearsman Books Ltd Registered Office
30–31 St. James Place, Mangotsfield, Bristol BS16 9JB
(this address not for correspondence)

www.shearsman.com

ISBN 978-1-84861-280-8

Copyright © Deborah Meadows,
2003, 2004, 2005, 2006, 2007, 2009, 2010, 2011, 2013.

The right of Deborah Meadows to be identified as the author of this work
has been asserted by her in accordance with the
Copyrights, Designs and Patents Act of 1988.
All rights reserved.

Cover image:
'Nightingale Sound Print, Heart Sound Print Over Ancient Calligraphy'
by Deborah Meadows

Contents

Prefatory Note	9
Acknowledgments	11

FROM *Representing Absence*
    Faux translation of Charles Baudelaire's "To the Reader"   15
    The Theory of Subjectivity in Moby-Dick

Invocation	17
Chapter 1	18
Chapter 2	20
Chapter 4	21
Chapter 6	22
Chapter 13	23
Chapter 14	24
Chapter 18	25
Chapter 20	26

FROM *Itinerant Men*
    The Theory of Subjectivity in Moby-Dick

Chapter 26	29
Chapter 27	31
Chapter 33	32
Chapter 37	33
Chapter 41	35
Chapter 46	37
Chapter 47	38
Chapter 48	39
Chapter 51	41

FROM "*The 60's and 70's:* from
    The Theory of Subjectivity in Moby-Dick"
The Theory of Subjectivity in Moby-Dick

Chapter 66	45
Chapter 68	46
Chapter 69	47

FROM *Itinerant Men* (continued)
The Theory of Subjectivity in Moby-Dick
        Chapter 80   51
        Chapter 89   52
        Chapter 92   53
        Chapter 102   54
        Chapter 110   56
        Chapter 114   57

FROM *Thin Gloves*
The Theory of Subjectivity in Moby-Dick
        Chapter 124   61
        Chapter 126   62
        Chapter 127   63
        Chapter 128   64
Gargant 1-6, 8, 23, 28-29, 36-37, 48-49, 50-51   65
Guest   81

FROM *Growing Still*   87

FROM *involutia*
    Luce Studies the Blue Cliff Record, a little opera   103
    Gilles Studies the Blue Cliff Record, a little opera   111
    Animated States   114
    Midnight in Our Motivated   116
    Necessary Truths   118
    Pets   120

FROM *Goodbye Tissues*
    American Possessions   127
    Goodbye Tissues   131
    Aquinas: *division textus*   135
    after Hölderlin   139
    Further Articles   140
    On Goodness in General   142
    Four   147
    Coda   154

FROM *Depleted Burden Down*
    Procuratio   159
    Early Soviet Cinema   169
    Translation, the bass accompaniment   173
    Arrival   175
    Another Interview   176
    Apotropaic Shuffle   178

FROM *Saccade Patterns*
    Keep, a Melodrama   189
    Threadwaste   190
    Opercula, fall off as they open   192
    School for Perisarcous Considerations   205
    How, the means   211
    where, a site index   225
    With hand on joystick   227
    Weak as a directive, no   229

Lamb Notes   230

Biographical Note   235

Dedicated to Howard

Prefatory Note

The bass guitar creates patterns that make music into a visceral experience—they are what infect the body. The poems in *Translation, the bass accompaniment: Selected Poems* are in dialog with other authors, and here, experimental poetry engages logician Quine, encyclopedic novelist Melville, philosophers Irigaray and Deleuze, theologian and synthetic philosopher Aquinas, poets Dragomoshchenko, Hejinian, Raworth, Baudelaire, and Celan, Soviet cinematographer Vertov, video artist Bill Viola, and others.

Many have written of the mediated experience that language, private life, and civic life involve. In that spirit, the poetry engages the syntax of exploratory thought from ten earlier books brought together here for the first time and ends with a poem that hints at a version of tomorrow.

I arranged *Translation, the bass accompaniment: Selected Poems* chronologically with two exceptions. The long work entitled 'The Theory of Subjectivity in Moby-Dick' is comprised of 135 chapters that were published across these locations: Green Integer's *Representing Absence* and *Thin Gloves*, Tinfish Press's "*The 60's and 70's: from The Theory of Subjectivity in* Moby-Dick," Krupskaya Press's *Itinerant Men*, and *Jacket* magazine. I departed from the chronological arrangement with the placement of excerpts from the Tinfish chapbook entitled "*The 60's and 70's: from The Theory of Subjectivity in* Moby-Dick" that here intersect Krupskaya's *Itinerant Men* because I thought the chapters are better read in sequence. The second exception is the placement of excerpts from 'Growing Still' written after the *Moby-Dick* sequence, yet through a fluke in publishing came out at an earlier date.

The books that follow that portion (*involutia*, *Goodbye Tissues*, *Depleted Burden Down*, and *Saccade Patterns*) are separate books yet mesh in other ways—political critique, philosophical exploration, interest in public and private speech, the durable mystery of translation, a look into the underlying assumptions of lived life, ethical thought, our troubled history, and the fragile nature of truth.

I am grateful to the many publishers who committed to and first produced my work, and for extending their permission. They include:

Douglas Messerli (Green Integer Press), Susan Schultz (Tinfish Press), Jocelyn Saidenberg (Krupskaya Press), Tony Frazer (Shearsman Books), Joel Kuszai (Factory School), Guy Bennett (Mindmade Books), and Geoffrey Gatza (BlazeVOX [books]). 'Lamb Notes' was published in *Stone Canoe: A Journal of Arts, Literature and Social Commentary.*

Deborah Meadows,
Los Angeles, 2012

Acknowledgments

These segments first appeared in the following books:
Representing Absence (Green Integer, 2004) from *The Theory of Subjectivity in Moby-Dick* Invocation and Chapters 1, 2, 4, 13, 14,18, 20, and Faux translation of Charles Baudelaire's "To the Reader;" *Itinerant Men* (Krupskaya Press, 2004) from *The Theory of Subjectivity in Moby-Dick* Chapters 26, 27, 33, 37, 41,46,47, 48, 51, 80,89, 92, 102, 110, 114 ; "*The 60's and 70's*: from *The Theory of Subjectivity in Moby-Dick*" (Tinfish Press, 2003) from *The Theory of Subjectivity in Moby-Dick* Chapters 66, 68, 69; *Thin Gloves* (Green Integer, 2006) from *The Theory of Subjectivity in Moby-Dick* Chapters 124, 126, 127, 128, Gargant 1-6, 8, 23, 28-29, 36-37, 48-49, 50-51, Guest; *Growing Still* (Tinfish Press, 2005) excerpts from *Growing Still*; *involutia* (Shearsman Books, 2007) excerpts from Luce Studies the Blue Cliff Record, a little opera, Gilles Studies the Blue Cliff Record, a little opera, Animated States, Midnight in Our Motivated, Necessary Truths, Pets; *Goodbye Tissues* (Shearsman Books, 2009) excerpts from American Possessions, Goodbye Tissues, Aquinas: *division textus*, after Hölderlin, Further Articles, On Goodness in General, Four, Coda; *Depleted Burden Down* (Factory School, 2009) excerpts from Procuratio, Early Soviet Cinema, Translation, the bass accompaniment, Arrival, Another Interview, Apotropaic Shuffle; excerpts from *How, the means* first appeared as a chapbook (Mindmade Books, 2010) and then was included in *Saccade Patterns* (BlazeVOX, 2011) along with Threadwaste, Opercula, fall off as they open, School for Perisarcous Considerations, where, a site index, With hand on joystick, Weak as a directive, no. Lamb Notes first appeared in *Stone Canoe: A Journal of Arts, Literature and Social Commentary.* Sources for *Saccade Patterns* include: Wikipedia entries on Head-up display and Synthetic Vision system, the *Compact O.E.D.*, *Threadwaste* by Robert Morris, *Engines of Logic: Mathematicians and the Origin of the Computer* by Martin Davis, *Frank Zappa, Captain Beefheart and the Secret History of Maximalism* by Michel Delville, *Pi in the Sky: Counting, Thinking, and Being* by John D. Barrow, and *Primates and Philosophers: How Morality Evolved* by Frans De Waal.

In addition to the book-length works acknowledged above, many of the poems, some in a slightly different form first appeared in the following books, anthologies, and various poetry publications:
  A Best of Fence: *The First Nine Years, American Letters & Commentary, Another Language – Poetic Experiments in Britain and North America, Antennae, Argotist, Boog City: A Community Newspaper From A Group Of Artists And Writers Based In And Around New York City's East Village, Burnside Review, Calculator, Calculate, Don Guillermo's Good Book: University of New Orleans post-Katrina anthology,* Electronic Poetry Center--Author Page <http://epc.buffalo.edu/authors/meadows/>, *Fascicle, Fence, Fourteen Hills: The SFSU Review, Generator,*

Generator's "Best of *Generator*" CD-ROM, *La Alteración del Silencio: Poesía Norteamericana Reciente* (Das Kapital Press, Santiago, Chile), *Los Rollos Del Mal Muerto* (Buenos Aires: in Spanish translation), *Mirage #4*, *Moria Poetry Journal, New Review of Literature, Plebella: Revista De Poesía Actual* (Buenos Aires: in Spanish translation), *Poets Against the War* site, *Poets For Living Waters, Pom2, Shearsman Magazine, Stone Canoe: A Journal of Arts, Literature and Social Commentary, The Brooklyn Rail: Critical Perspectives on Arts, Politics, and Culture, The PIP Anthology of World Poetry of the 20th Century,* volume 5, *Intersections: Innovative Poetry in Southern California, The PIP (Project for Innovative Poetry) Blog, The Poker, Tinfish Magazine, 3,785 Page Pirated Poetry Anthology, Zoland Poetry: An Annual of Poems, Translations & Interviews,* and as an exhibit of poetry translated into Spanish in large-format for the 2007 visual arts show "Third Anniversary of *Plebella: Revista De Poesía Actual*" in the National Library of Argentina.

from

Representing Absence

Faux translation of Charles Baudelaire's 'To the Reader'

The sot, his error or fishing lens
lives in our spirits, works in our bodies,
so we eliminate our friendly notes
like mendicants nourishing our vermin.

Our fish are heady, our repentance milky.
We do ourselves gross injustice by what we have
and lease happiness in a scarlet shirt.
Known for its dye that runs when washed, we touch it.

On the topic of bad birds, there's thirteen
who longs for our impress, our service,
whose baton will vaporize all our freedom
like a suave atomic scientist.

It's the bull who has our reconstructed son!
About the repulsive objects we work on, we joke
about the day the flames of our descendants are not about here
we joke without bleakness in order to cross the sills that leak.

The poor debauched sot who lowers his mouth and eats
the martyred river from an antique cupboard
we go together along a passage of pleasure and secrecy
that is hard pressed like our agent's orange.

Zig-zag yet still being formed by millions of hemoglobin donors
is the cut womb of the townspeople
and when we breathe death itself into our lungs,
we breathe the invisible flowers very deeply of our sad songs.

If Viola, poison, flowery painters, and revolutionaries
are not brooding again and again over their demented pleasures,
then the everyday canvas of our pitiful destiny
is our friend like a hell that can't be hardy.

But the old images in the canyons, the mountain lions and bugs,
the chanters, scorpions, and biting snakes
are all monstrous exaggerations of those that are merchandized
at ramparts of our notorious zoo of cruelty and vice.

It is more laid, more sold, more unworldly
than anything else that can be a large gesture or big cry.
It volunteers the garbage of the land
and lowers all our attempts in this world.

The eye of the bored person involuntarily blinks
because it dreams of the sot high from smoking.
You know it's true, that monstrous delicacy,
that drug of hypocrisy, like me, like you.

The Theory of Subjectivity in *Moby-Dick*

Invocation

    … ous author

the truth, let us do
            let us correct the way
it miscarried the primitive

for a deviant, at first delay

       come home
       things are due

The   … ous author

Clear the whole
Clear where you wrote "that and what"

No blood is good blood
purchased with a Franklin.

all confess to whole adventures.

      *

Chapter 1

Having little or no subjectivity
brought into the world carrying cargo
or amor or moral precept to the street.

Mount it high, this substitute for piracy
sought and Lenten, mid-town is the Bath
pooled and previous
Were lovers there
some afternoons?

Avenues, when awkward, peep, but the
haunches and plaster tied to what is gone:
   How are the needles?
Once marketed for drakes, take whims
or experiments: metaphysical procedures
wedded to You (subjectivity, again)

The dreary sleep in the governor's cottage
amazing us with handfuls of silence,
refusals of purpose:
   Why did the pillar go to brother's?
   Must hearsay against others define Us?

Will Narcissus result in carnage, we should
shout that something is said about Image.
   A purse is passé, don't general things
or something of everykind whatsoever say "myself."

      Call me.

      *

     Of you. The topic in miniatures
& shards. Their huge night behind them
when "I," so to speak, "go to sea,"
I go by the royal dumb-down in the foyer
to make rosy shadows. Of you.

The tallest assume "you" with concoctions
of identity, but ever-alert, what about
-roon blood, old sea captains, cup & punch,
other kinds of servants of metaphysical
trouble?

Whereas, "you" are never heard of.

     *

Constant.
Constant stands alone, free in pure air of stern
axioms far more private for their
atmosphere, Pythagorean violations.
Their stink of Fate that dogs me.

What better Whole is bloody as those stagnant
parts of circumstances which being
curated means the state, the ship
of state, Constant.

     *

Chapter 2

Reaching
inhaled reaching, followed by or tucked
in as most stop at this place.

A place of departure where headrests, sleep,
originals are required: cement
banisters merge public and private lives,
how can order disguise the bows, bowsprits, etc.

Frost lay. I said to myself, as towards
identity and self-naming, lower your bag
and cover the darkness toward
expensive pavements and pumice the
secret inwardness. It's all self, all
society, dreary streets and buses on from
here and hereafter. Moving
absorbs many of the works in public, so
encased in ashes, in poor boxes.

A common place. I muttered bathetic
entertainment by the weeping negro church.
I suppose I might look enough, seem
sufficient that tenting indoors, that judgment
more than ever divides. Matchless
is the miracle on the outside where the
window frosts only one-way. Northern
lights raise the dead man within, silken his
pillow lengthwise.
Now fiery, more of this scrape and plenty.

*

Chapter 4

Made of patchwork, this self
interminable squares and palimpsest scrivened
language.

        As a procedure
to fill or to empty: my mother of circumstances,
this sea of scholarly conditions and strange
questions contribute to the misfortune
of selfhood, punning at the window
with blankets and the sound of a house
going from bad to worse—at last
I got circular in the garden, steeped
in trouble.
        It's a Norm, was a norm
straining through horrid days.
Fear of possession, "mine" were,
I'm very sure. As if what he did, on the "savage's
side" of patchwork is a baby; unruly,
thought I. Debased in the offing of
my mind, he came to nothing about
conclusions or quandary quietly. Upon
narratives, he understood, but the
truth essentially went nameless, a man
always well worn with probability. It's
cultural: was a creature in the butterfly
in the strangest possible location or
was he just another pinch in the morning?
Seeing this plainly as arms and
washed as a wooden stock, we are
restricted by the stride, its length, its
series we come to know. How exceeding
the edge defines it as a proud monkey
of counting.

        *

Chapter 6

Daylight. Daylight lends an exoticizing
vision, this quotidian street with
wealth hauled up from capitalized
seas to widow walks, flowers festooned
upon Nature's bare rock with great Art.
In Bedford the frequent foreigner
stands athirst for gain. Experience
mocks Innocence descended from sweet
farm land, even overly precious
ideas of self will be tested, and, no
doubt, found wanting, stripped down
by Tempest-force winds.

Fame. A famous town where bumpkins
mow their notoriety short, where a court
makes great fear of forged blades
in this land whose condition is more than ever
opulent for grand givers of dowries that
even horse chestnut trees show "candles" just
for those few powerful men for
whom all creation must be cut
down, boiled, rendered to a distillate
of consolidated selfness. Small towns,
sweet by appearance, destroy what fugitive
kind they don't understand, and knowledge
by formula cannot complete
its desire to comprehend all. The young,
the green, the swallowing machine.

*

Chapter 13

The boarders wheel a device to become
adventurers across cultural theories
about every person adjusted having
"seen me," particular affects, stuff
that is well-tried in the heart. For example,
one of yours came to our wedding
to the place he has never seen; it was
a calabash, lent him from the boarding
house, both ornamental and
punctilious, used in certain grand, solemn
occasions: the commandeer, the King,
the Grace. Self placed next to or into
the bowl makes quick foam.

And so. Huge hills, world-waves while
friends and slender acquaintances lay
silent and safely glide beyond her
wharves, and somehow "I" spurn or
factor dented records on slavery.
Understood as indelible, these seas,
their greenness must endure. Jeering our
past, tasks aboard this gaunt rib of the
sea ask: what do you mean by that?
Is hatred, conflict and prejudice
the low flying part of the main-sail,
roughly washed, sent toward the lower
jaw, being done, the boom whipped
all the safety into an example of
totality while the hands connect by feel,
bulwarks sensed as solid, weighty, a few
minutes more with the other, the mutual
human joined in aid through form restored
as difference.

*

Chapter 14

Our map. As packet or subset, this
dune is a scale of knowing, a collection
of exaggerated observations, puns on toothpicks
to lumberjacks. Extravaganzas of place,
origin in bird flight, in sea hunt:
at it a long time, years as a bell
you see more than hear, three blades
of conquest, a shade of colonial hours
made of grass, made mistaken,
perennial intention.

They were malicious: where some take rags
in tow, they barrel their moss. Fond, at last,
of watery trade, they first caught
plankton, then graduated to eohippus
as they waded out, then pushed off in
boats arranged to capture oceanic
wealth, power, and multiple meanings
attributed to whales.

Despite sea hernias,
they conquered sub-surface plantations,
divided among pirate powers, even poetry
the bogeymen of the Rose. Land like
lines, armed on the left-hand side following
the dictates of business which had
overwhelmed all courtships, fellowships,
and other ships such as Earth that feckless
gull our sunset buckets west between
billows so at sea it is.

*

Chapter 18

Fear takes the shark to Judgment who
ain't a pretty shark. Tell me, who on
board in the fierce cognate of the killer
paradigm sent the sea breaking Death
and his house?

Mending a top sail offered the counterpart:
how those who make their mark
are subordinated by those who sign
their names. Thus it has been "our
Duty" eyeing the inferior systems of
hicks and hogs. A trade bead. The great
church doesn't know anything about
the way you were born. Creation
and destruction of a small drop of tar,
kinship stepped on women—each
bead most simple in its relation
so the state can cry out
in some such way, pamphlet over,
declare terms: Name is Event.

Previous. The cannibal author on the wharf
delineates sequence as a postulate leaning
forward, taking out spectacles
to rub clean like a member.

*

Chapter 20

Employed with housekeeping of the world:
beds, saucepans, chests, the usual as well as
specialty equipment. Necessary material
culture, hurrying bankers, an old
lady, pension, and loss of the very
truths on which society most
depends. Her impenetrable space,
the success of runes and radio telemetry,
no spare captain, the heaviest gauge
harpoons. Indefatigable crew members
dissolved beneath the sudden drop
of a promise to contact others on board.
It all runs backward; falling lanceward
could compare over and over.

Out upon the green during these days
of Ahab, the draft not getting between
the two as often as the suspects
alone or solitary. When he was going through
the motions, I held suspicions
but said nothing inventive.

*

from

Itinerant Men

Chapter 26

To: swart commoner of fire, our
shipped and paupered artist who God
didst give uncommon craft from
one Spirit of Equality.

I, the writer, writes "noble" and "royal
mantle of humanity" to instruct
my fellow countrymen lifting language
      to this new instance
whether errors of an eye,
man glowing with remains of an ideal,
the ordinary irrational struggle
      (fear of the whale Starbuck
          requires, never hunting after sun-
down) menace you from the centre
and circumference of flesh
      not as fearful as the dignity of divine
or spiritual terror
      not as tragic as the undoing of goodness
in our Starbuck.

Estimation conducted in ignorance is, at times, the
visual field, can outdo far away or ceded instances
of human room to the rain of utter cowards
careful, Aye, with the business of the ship.
Wasted minor lowerings that never sting
a fish in recessed deeps, we ask: could
he see what he saw?

Latitudes baked our adapted biscuits
boiled like books whose author steps out
to be general in address drowned with
character-identity, yea addresses
God that we can overhear! Contingent

fit and poor health to come under
torrid Sun unworshipped by staid,
steadfast anti-knights in their
pantomime of action.

     *

Chapter 27

A state of all-knowing provokes a return
to life.

Brains and unbrains divide the federated
nations aboard socially.

Our grievances come back before
grim time.

Corporeal as a binary, he volunteered
as brawn for this chessboard.

Intimacy between first and second: one
steps forward, two fills that space in battle,
forces descend in hosts of what it means
to be "in companies."

Mouths, hand, succession
of movements, you have consumption. Disinfect
the vine dead to any encounter or, at
least, become small as a carpenter's
nail, Flask. Crisis collected at leisure
and long usage might be a way to humor
the motives of Stubb. Who invites us here to
learn from an omniscient point of view?

*

Chapter 33

        not their social equal, my Captain
of democracy.

        "famous through infinite inferiority,"
        requires "imperial purple," not pilot cloth

"the aid of external arts and entrenchments,"
"so plebeian herds crouch abased
      before triumphant centralization"

Empire steps godly and leaps Soho
now become pumice hidden load by load.
Our ringed crowd of plebeians doubt
civilization carries an indomitable
hint. Dregs and housing stock
mingle in thee. Its studied air.

To beget terror, our captain is given
to that indulgence about which nothing
can be spoken. Instantaneous with shoes,
others are lodged in the aft taking
their meals at His Table. A voyage
seeps unknown or Unknown
centuries. Wholly the class of whale-men
largely depends upon an important
office or minor dignity.

              *

Chapter 37

Soliloquy.
A device to
speechify inner life. A
dramatization, often relying
on elevated poetic language to
identify binary divisions of friend
and foe, past and present, whole and
reduced selves, overly grand placement
in the world and elevated purpose or mission.
Largely discarded by twentieth century
writers or replaced by a letter, an
overheard therapy session, an
overheard conversation
or argument with
lover, cell mate,
partner
in
plan.

*

    See not its
    white and long waters
    that close behind
        my large
        passage
    A gentle swerve,
    I wear not gold,
    my brow is mine.

    Power, damned
    in the midst of Paradise

and one stubborn
        blinded

prizefighter, or if you will
that self-sound
before me, and I try
to match itself
with "must" and
"necessity" but
        maddened
by lists and schoolboys
        I've run
naught to pommel *me*
nor from me.

        *

Chapter 41

On historic and mythic sources.

                                              … ous author

Cause my soul, greedy with existence,
other circumstances, other malice
than the monster. Featured in sailor gossip,
calamities and
                    fabulous
rumors, featured in expert report as
                    ferocious,
                    ubiquitous.
A white whale inspired
                    curious
speculation about its terrible vocation that
                    superstitious
hunters and erudite research
meet beneath the surface, even
finding the Nor'West Passage, our
                    fabulous
whales know more than underground men.
In ships floating near a whale
that had been known for intelligent malice,
                    treacherous
authors chew on six inch blades,
the prior chapter's knife fight
lessened in contrast to Ahab abob
with the Thing whose
                    malicious
agencies eat at heart, liver, limb.

        *

Subtle demonisms, Ahab, his hidden self,
his debased rational will a mere instrument,
the old man's Horn swells, his narrow
                              righteous
soul crushed by inner self, mad intention
deployed by sane Means;
                              audacious
revenge through utility of plan
                              unconscious
of hiswriterly fatality.

                *

Chapter 46

That one far too wedded opens.

That he hunted there, his soul elsewhere.

Considerations may still tender knowable aspects.

Their long night may lapse into rebellion
        anticipated by "prudential" leaders.

All influences bear upon significance
and falsity.

Crying out for moderation,
        our manufactured man
has appetites and futile conditions.

Drawn to usurpation, work together.
Swerved from its ultimate course,
        a wing suspended.

        *

Chapter 47

Yet mundane repetitions
        set up the Loom of Time.

The mat and I-myself crosswise
        to necessity: my hand
        in service to the machine.

My own tiny weavings,
unutterable threads seem done-
side of freely made.

Dropped from high: alternate way
        to restricted accident, free
        from its ultimate threads, suspended
high ego like a war tending toward
strategy, concerted movement.

        Blows like a clock.
The Indian confidently looked
        toward that singular section,
secretly headed inward
        expectant atoms formed there.

        *

Chapter 48

Called the devil to account

but silly protrusions omit. D'ye hear
black cotton reply to agents on the water?

Lay back for command, erect help, indenture.
Rascals softly give way to yellow.

Time looked indolent; others inculcate
        broad manias like an odd sort of charm.

Whisper not a single word to lash men onward.

Small measure, their wonder. Five trip-hammers,
        all steel and flesh, appearance and conjecture.

The chase.

Whales' irregular spacing—

Also triangular, then tip us up and
        didn't pause, then the eye of it
        down in the blue movement
of the sunk world, then harmonious solace
once received by me, and vivacious attitude
now receiving.

                *

"The bearer looked nobler than the rider."

The crew detached flying from its element,
        four puffs of vapor.

Then harsh water, head far off,
        fell to loss of purpose,
          pursuit and its canvas

in these critical moments

        a repeated spectacle up to gunwales,
        vast swells upon her, emotions
pull into the charmed Design
        like cries whispered by hand.

Something rolled, collapsed through
        erected crests. Our whole mortal
work unconsumed, then muffled, then continued
        around ropes, feet, pole, hope, heart.

We swam.

                        *

Chapter 51

Watery location, the racks, waves, scrolls
of silver, suffused seethings, glittering god.

Dense accentuation giving onto trochees:
You will harken sightings here.

Limb sound whenever, wherever
        the lifting tendency follows
        sailors' falling: one, two,
        die or do.

Howling around us.

Strange forms recede from all that space
        vacating itself,
        the perfidious nature
        of beckoning
as if Something is there

inscrutable as a conscience.

The anguish of fatalists loosened
some time before—glad humanity
        swung
in response or accustomed hole.

        *

from

"The 60's and 70's *from*
'The Theory of Subjectivity in *Moby-Dick*'"

Chapter 66

In the present, any man
unaccustomed to business
        may here learn how
completely common
and entirely necessary is
        massacre. Were he
a skeleton present on, say,
a morning we process
        a corpse, by evening

no reservation felt toward images,
        representations of Hell.
Internees are prodded by spades
their intestines swallowed
by self and each other, voided so
        who is who
        incessantly murdering
by striations struggling
        deep in their skulls'
vital confusion.
Our commodity meddles
        with reality; scene
might be called mutual
        with its frame.

        *

Chapter 68

Skin remains a question:
"what and where is the skin of the whale?"

What and where is the mind?
        Inscribed upon, see through
        a brittle clarity, read through spectacles
that make a skin
over skin.

Upon the printed page or
        written into flesh as
warm-blooded as "we"
yet indecipherable.

Quarters for a child
        assuming one more tender
        than skin—
bulk mysterious, yet
        phenomena present how
        rocks connect
        to pyramids, as made things.

Borneo
man of nature, specimen body
with skin parsed for warmth.
Specimen-skin made, marked, for sale.

Comfortable with risk, copied
        to dominant collection of twoness
dispersed by instruments
        identical
to how small easy pieces
can be rendered
and teach these fine creatures how.

        *

Chapter 69

I am nearly lost in this panorama.

Still colossal except the insatiate surface
          on which plays whale reduction.

                Mock funeral screams
lie where flesh represents
waste, where illustration-told
opens space onto fiction.

Further from the ship, the ghost whale
          creates "presence," its representation
          floats in the mind for years,
so shun the place, and in so doing
          make tradition, mark orthodoxy.
Geographic "sheep leap over a vacuum"
          that lies where the reduced poem
          represents excess, where illustration-told
forecloses place onto strange love.

                    *

from

Itinerant Men
(continued)

Chapter 80

Brain-nut resting elsewhere
          hidden within
outerworks, a fort in Quebec,

I have a casket
peremptorily squared.

                        Indications
of audacity relieved by phrenological
          comparisons:
                        spinal branch
of philosophy.

          "This august hump"
almost equal to the map
of some indomitable
                reason.

        *

Chapter 89

Whole of the law.
Fair game, the bankrupt, discounted
       loans, fey application
       rightly so.

Broken-back laborers, women,
Ireland, Mexico:
          litigated
in set terms, property
is our wife
       or another man's
cited case, subsequent
gentleman's harpoon and line
       factored in commentaries
as high moral injustice
inspired by a fast-fish
       lashed boatside, so
expresses *intention*
that holy abstraction, will-to-own
       alive or dead
symbol and badge applicable
       to lawyers cruising
universal escape
partaking terse
          applications,
encoded contingencies.

       *

Chapter 92

                    ...music unsaxed by course of air, stopped.
Amber found, ambergris for substance,
        frankincense flavored our four boat loads.
Perfume from putridity, the postulate

fractures pouf, parlor pretension
with *observed truth.*

Compound motives with cultural clutter
to repel bias
        as corruption stinks
        to capital C.
Decay is nothing, is not nothing
        by way of business
        arisen from foundation
of national smell.

Possibly—furnaces and fat-kettles
        seldom please
a musk-scented lady more than
        operations enjoyed
out of phase, that famous elephant
        fricative exercise?

                *

Chapter 102

Unbutton further our Euro-traipse
      unto other science, now oarsmen
privilege one Jonah
      his *unconditional skeleton.*
Female animation
      has opportunity to witness,
dissect all inlaid structures.

Remember Banquo, our foil,
beside palm leaf villa
      where "I was invented"
native island of *natural* cast:
trading ribs, branding,
affrighted dinner guests.

High and haughty without
the fabric of words, pause
or fly from carpets of ceaseless
      deception. Ah, the mortal word
involved you in skull studies
      placed before this plough.
Wood shaped by toil, mordant
by edge.

Yard sticks, I quickly concluded,
      measure superior lengths
throughout stories of whispering
galleries, echo the hollow-chest
of anatomical compilation made
for moderate England.
I had them tattooed
      right here, left
the rest of me blank.

My body, congenial
to odd inches, new poems.

*

Chapter 110

On interpretation. Its tantalizing aspects.

From a gigantic slumber
      our coffin drawn from puncheons
and placards, casks and quips,
demijohn and head in hand goes
      to dinner in catacombs
      that resound with emptied
      vocations, danger in woolen drawers,
half disemboweled thighway yet spotted
      from hatchways on rolling frames
by mere bystanders to fevers' invisible flood.

      Like those that fancy a canoe,
he ordered accuracy, promptitude,
ruled measure forthwith,
      rationalized boat of death
transferred accurately as paddles' consort
      with humorous cries within Queequeg,
a bag of mortal views
ring a hammock's sway.

      I say "game" not ancient tongue
spoken by lofty scholars, delirium
can fit coward to general, rally
preparatory faith in matter of certainty,
      texts inscrutable to theory
or mystical treatise.

To copy text from text: a departure
      from graphic marks to truths that turn
on poise and difference. Can makers
      know sense of their senses?

      *

Chapter 114

When certain filigrees smooth
our canoe with filiations
or fill our hold with hidden bodies
        tears are rovers' barracoes.

Soothing scenes, temporary effects
        make orphan, phantom limb, nation
            possessed of sinister
pain, an apparition of extremities,
        branches of horror tree.

Nor may mast or caste form
one seamless mood however
        temporal, so that ever-theoretical
our mingled threads, our mothers
die, fathers disappear, our weary
fail at progress in neighborhoods'
        norms, dreary as faith
in worms, ousted facts, teeth-tiered
        variables—faith: our surface.

    *

from

Thin Gloves

Chapter 124

Read a turned needle
        before the bayonet
        of yellow demanding
reason. Shakily Baconian

in its juncture of superstition
and science, ships in view of magnetic
        deliberation ranged abroad
        more than the Pequod.

The old East, an institution, hence
        go into that if assessed. The pole
as certain space, mentality,
a provision Ahab handed to his crew
as a stroke of congenial mastery.

The pole wiped Ahab of triumph
settled in place
at either binary extreme.
Over *one* quivers *one*
        onto the round
where Ahab met Ahab.

        *

Chapter 126

Frequency.

Strange wind, dying calm,
        trade wild for carved Romans.
Ahab did not hesitate to deck Christians
        with non; peculiar tones coming
from water fall from faces
        in a heap. Structure of portent:

        an evil in the future,
mounted thus, for they declared
        circumstances, reading
a seal's cry, broken cord,
        drowned sailor.

The lid implies body as witness
        to cobbling "beneath"
carpenters; dignity balks
at buoyed air, eclipsed signs of late.
        His coffin can endure
bedsteads I forgot—no caps
        at sea nor job-shop,
stash, or lee. One speaker
displays local pikes abroad.
Novel structure
                cyclopic or
encyclopedic?

        *

Chapter 127

On the state of the novel as a coffin.

Fiendish old scamps
had clapped enough
to institutionalize their tapping.

From cabin to shop, believe in
       sufficient music, in caulking
or sounding out the unpronounceable.
       Hark, all things come right
with a test upon waters for central
lines, radiant riggings.

"How immaterial are all materials,"
ticked time beats against
the hollow structure of measured time.

Philosophies benight me
as things I do more conducive
to symbol as turpentine is
to carpenters' plans in twilight
conduits from this world
       for which we measure
stilts and pier piles, moorings, marks.

*

Chapter 128

Rachel descending.
        What late converse upon
        this stranger's boat goes?
        Windward blare
upon a wooden hull.
                      The Pequod expired,
a man aloft far from pretension
in sweeping search for the Whale,
        for the sons fed to industry; long
practice, so criminal origin
        eludes factual recall, still wagering
pale in the very myths, lowered
version, common sense, ethical call:
        greatest good for the greatest wretched.

Anger must save that boy, all
        of ye heard seals and lost sailors
shortly placed prior to reason—
        nor do wonders and other phenomena
        occur spawned by unwarranted returns
        to our binnacle watch.

              *

Gargant

after Rabelais

Note: Derived from a version of the 'Gargantua' section of François Rabelais' volume *Gargantua and Pantagruel,* first published in 1534, that was translated by two late 17th century persons, Sir Thomas Urquhart and Pierre Le Motteux, (Everyman's Library, 1994).

Calls to be more faire
>   hold what they knew
>   oil of sense & surl

Marrow of doctrine
>   attains
>   picto-flourish
phantasmagorical
>   symbol
>   of
>   anatomy
>   of
>   conscience

pious gullet
good valve
>   rend meaning Selves
>   serious things
>   to say about diligence
>   accoutered

as incredible goats, their lives,
>   seen in shadowed
>   pantheist
>   Simples.

        1

The former time—
           inelectable as certain pants
           an Emperor,
born of desires
      masked in authored
books was struck against
      in sluices
unfrozen from tombs made
      by nocturnal pamphlets
some had nibbled, so
      complicated a reading.

2

"Anti-onumated…
           conc-etter…"
is almost said
       some of his prelators
look on arms and eaters
       gaping through gaps
holo-grams of Cy-sores
       unless

Cleare, short, flat ideas
       cath-olving such a jeer-shed
no more catching fallow guys
       unlesse

working for Hawthorne Brews,
       burne one sign to save
minc-aves from their riches
       that dic-lost, we com-kers
sweat close for
       "Hell or hell-aster"
the swung bell could while.

                3

Three gargantuan months late
        a notable jester, "I" was then intent

bastard
custard
mustard
muster the Green
        of Lombardy Links,
a skin-stouffed width
        that Jupiter made a bit later.

Nay, hunger queargues
salacious as ancien-increase.
        Enquirer on the ladle
of ballast & lading,
        labor without pari-danger

can finde
their husbande
                hoisted in liber-humous;
sachems kept the paupican state
        very weened
never an heir so meat,
        macrobial, stop-not
                concrease.

4

How tripe a yeare,
        fruit of beeves
men lickt
        noche-kers
a year and fourteen.

Debilitated but tall,
        Boud-rillos stiff
as casing for three bushels
        standing, O.

5

Mon mot, I wet
        by scancioned flablets
the charity of flagons' ting, glaze
with water a thirst, not a charicere,

        hither a word-moth fly:
I amongst it, I kills it, I have rights.

When new and eager with normal
        exhalations called between boyles
and vice, be lusti-fruct
        Aime, a bouquet of soma-drink
to my turne like another corner
        of accentual lash appealing to gentle
& worried lustiness. Drifters made
        of dough-ards, ink the alkali
fiends, good as decoction
        of beasti-tar upon one ear
heighs mellif-land tones annulling.

6

Organs were plebeggarelles
        off the grate,
unwell but suspecting
        trouble. Spirits'
ell saying grievous vines.

Goat's blood from mum-meane
        -tire futures: I will be…
        I shall be…, then suddenly,
barroom tripes, from below
        her fundament (enmity
in the terrean) Saint Being
        issued forth
                not as other stuffe
both cleave to & cleave apart
        could not
Hubri-cock our idle spirits,
        it is at his hark
a woman-hence—
        which swindles more?

8

Breeches & arms ordained—
        ordinary as champs
of the gutter were those blew
        apparels. Damask

& diamond broidered cod piece
        corny as cornucopias. Decked

with gall, gallant as enamel
        the neck respective
and wood reaped for endurance
        two elated dreads
        counter, rather contradict
half-rejoycing others,
        set with market's Emerald—
a spire's height to crash
        at nine hundred.

23

Gordian to make by the hour, notably
        time-ected to perp-faire
these anti-cyrillics affect or augment waxed nights.

Syllabic fumes confer predication
        upon lumps of continuous speech.
Combed to praise, they may grow according
        to scallop-way or vector broken by dice.

Aristotle gave form munificence, Pollux
        went five-out with new inventions.
An Englishman who veerily hands cause
to the Ancients sundered Gymnasts who lift up
        a cuirassier saddle, carry male-coat to fleet horse

aire to high leap, table to rude point.

But these external movements, do they order
or shroud tack held like a book
        set just above waterline without wetting it?

Roused shot tried our fore-ouse, took
        helm and hill. Why must victors pomp
        and mentors champion passing good?
Hey, crepe stood profitable as personified death.
        Feet prayed: situation done, starred briefly.

28-29

Dear son,

>Should a soldiery skirmish pass fire
>>broiling ramps, athletic fathers…

For enormous abuses to heritable title
>move me to advise you, favorable
>counsel, honest subjects

subjected by Right, *I will not undertake warre,*
until I have first tried all wayes and means
of peace, that I resolve upon.

>The people follow a road to thee,
cause free-born spirits to offer free reason

>>good behaviour as military policy,

>>Thy Father

36-37

A robber's tree marks
        how giantism reduces enemies
to unpeopled-backwash: the famed Deluge
        of Mare urine.

Come, pass the castle.

A kernel, a hose choked with flies,
        imagism on a bough in the rain.

Grotesqueries & guts,
how very compatible—
        refined expression
with state-made death.

Voided entertainment, a ringbone-embraced
        bladder, "style" for grave-diggers.

Consume phoenixes and farm animals
        Samsons & Marilyns,
hold a toothsome bobble
        in a momentary tower of taste,

come out of variety then.

48-49

Defeated utterly, charge of Passe made
        unsel-nen, varied bough
        of women, order for man haptic
and and good, microcholeric in place,
        how might antediluvian cakes & valleys
reach their fellow monkeys?

        Pursuers advance, space besieged
synchronically, sallie out having shot
        their religion. Artillery fire near wall.

Can abandoned men know, attain, and fill
        the hereafter with hubris (withered, rare
        leafage sunk nobly then shit)?

Lordly, microhole gave hope to towne,
        written-sound fortunes. His choleric
horse shall be re-evaluated by hags
        incensed about sly munitions,
        their own humps desire.
                There,
        by month's pay a direction arose
                that remedies installment with drink.

50-51

Why have there been men for whose clemency
      speech, arches, barriers
remembrance of victor & vanquished
      were purchased?

                    Furious the region
of fried loads competing for creed, dogma
toward being, spices & civet-cats.
      Deliver your posterity now.

Persons profusely detained made sayings
      not equal to virtues made nil:
          "…that this warre was undertaken
against my will, and without any hope
to increase either my goods or renown…" (143)

      our Ponocrates, our Kissinger, our Powell,
        I am sorry.
Administration, on cue, covets facility
& confidence with
        checking & reprehending
        trouble

Praised & delivered as one bad-trash
    as farre as great antic
          goblets, candles, tasse,
Bowl in a clear rock
      so others…

Guest

Commentary after M. A. Screech

"The pets we had were actually my brothers."
—unattributed, draft essay

Pagan in fruit, shew
                beautiful form by stoic
                examination
certainly used to balance
scholars' misconceptions.

Hard on the system, ranges second
        cruciform standing
            between instinct & lector

Greek Deus early to answer
our opprobrium over interpolation
        of Plutarch, wing
in main details.

So we turn from passage to influence,
simple metaphysics to daemons more human
                come accounts
                    whose divinatory resumption
greets bona fide relevance
        spared comparison
in pax tropicana.

                *

These very influences lay then
      with the concept Rabelais
      rashly held for *hero*, Augustine encore,
grueling points to worry the ages.

      After the body encore: news,
clarity, statement of inherent
      mortality, serious problem
      of divinity.
                  Episode of gestation
who tells lamentable suppositions,
leap from logical trespass
to moral fuss.

The doctrine makes bigots of pagans.

Closely devoted to heroism, a eulogy by form.

The prior world of Pan should quote
      vengeance.

All the rest develop peculiarly
as hostile doctors, accepting lawyers
      stranded on allegorical fragments.

Why are wise exalted, found essential
      in standard accounts?

Spreading literature.

      *

-bbits adduce terminology studiously
    that make articles folly and dogma comic.

Here, a prohibition-inspired puzzle, interpretative
    enigma sourced as measure
    of social constraint.

That any petite thing really fits no longer
    a given, setting friend against link,
    obvious taken for clarity.

Who will scan the version now as vulgate
    verses, thought more interesting
    than tradition, gloss in parts, pieces.

If "I am" second, then closely…
    ours, it is remembered

*

Talk about what is behind
a hundred blades ensured
hollow iron
            real difference.

Other than outlandish chants, an
electric kiss replaces gift with rim
of understanding. Adam, his resemblance.

Sentimental ear, are you the gill
he has in mind as necessity
raises lines to new levels?

As if crossing sections
toward a pool depicted
sliding diligently toward bitten word.

            *

from

Growing Still

There are wells where even at noon the stars are sharp
But branching out like a book into strangeness—a possibility
                                        always remains,
sand
and standing still.
Some word, like law's mold, reveals the world reversed
                    mirrored down the axis of matter.
                                              And so
this peeling apart
in tireless trials of freedoms.

        from 'A Sentimental Elegy' by Arkadii Dragomoschenko,
            trans. Lyn Hejinian and Elena Balashova,
            Description (Sun & Moon, 1990)

Once, when two passed into many, a shifting ruse claimed heritage, when clandestine revolution offered a way to dwell in enunciative loveliness, liquid, accelerated speech. Marine life costumes itself to deceive and survive. Traditional in what can add to understanding, we read here decipherment. Piled stones of similar size, a theme worked uniformly. When did coherence displace constancy, meaning unseat duration? With what poor tools: chain, toothed wheels, spokes and links. Hopper, collecting pan, irony of how early clockmakers derive parts. In its smooth running the mechanism recedes behind culture, detoured by fragments of bone, farmed in even rows.

*

Had picked up illegible faces, then diminished signal. Material extra-neous to agrarian narrative theorized as founding of revelatory unseating, "a spill" or "detriment." Passage between: dead past looks out from paper backing where flecks of lit material exert presence. Had we not looked scientifically? Measured rainfall? An upward swing frustrates transfer of this material. Person, structure, sky. Just there, above rooflines, just the tip showing. Line of evidence, a way to mark time—fish pass. A school turns on a dime computing many then one. Our time, that props an unseated plinth with meaning, abstracted from a top heavy branch—complex, constant forest required by Hume's unreliable imagination. The way a horse became the measure, horse-power.

A third element devoted to successive ridges concocting *distance* from experience of world, repetition in dart and roll maneuvers, a swallow's zag. See, the irreducible band of flying insects, a legible zone, not our unbroken skies for a sentimental readership of birds. A bird was noticed, an alienation effect. He paid begging children to simply go away, yet on they followed. Outlines, mere surface fragments slip to patterns, the stratosphere torn narrowly by a fighter jet. Not passive voice.

*

This month: a charged symbol, anatomy of time. Leafage supposedly shows plan, or is it determined arc of gorgeous event? The arc of a bucket's rim, surface growing still, a person has patiently run, a trait of time with equal sides for mechanized measure. Here alternates with there in a child's game interpreted as source of invention, of withdrawal of sustenance. Invented this month, this year (a notation extends between two points adding burden of past to this month), we take weight against our shoulders for now.

The banal man from television re-set, a high concept art device. Is it too late to shock us from ambiguity? Waves cross, form temporary points a plot engine requires, then diminish. The foretaste of imagery, water's two-element formula.

*

Long years of war.

Drip by drop, a river passes our flimsy raft and passes between fingers that disrupt tensile drama washing themselves with what is already gone. Below: rats & cats. The harmonious bird defines *excess* precisely pushes one fledgling from the nest for good. Practical, never quite free from extraneous sandwiched tight against claims for purity. A bucket, a glass. Alternation needs *between*, a third term; needs sequence, a war on stilled shots between frames. Brimming with same and same, abstractions pass, weave, are figurative across the surface sheeting over the edge of falls, and, against evidence of planar movement conceive origin grounded in passage of time, advocating inner against outer, failed flight dominated by significance.

This month gets repeated: slapped cards played for conveyance across rivers, a ritual coiled tight for peace. But how can predecessors gamble with our valuables? Did things sum differently, plants bend under newer stars along a riven repetition that was always there, a human vice? A freighted meaning, symmetry, from these worn seats flickered here, moth-like, holding things things holding, theatre-style.

*

Little time left. Incongruous to dress as usual, to spoken usage, a fond familiar neck. Metal clicks subside as stove contracts, variable heat having risen from glittering glaze to new status marked by recurrence, accretion of fittingness, sheer weight of iron, its image in the eye's meridian. No startled collapse of dimensions beneath weight of hand compressing a tiny bird tinier, its iridescent throat made resident in photographs, yet never wholly captured in human dimension, its properties rarely repeated, to a miner his distinguished taste in rock, ground of apparent universe, let into a grammatical shell surface of oily coffee found by accident.

Insistence upon using correct terms despite the infrequency of interlocutors, sketchy outlines of technique becoming bookish in the mind. Work. Work with long-handled shovel, a mental game of grammatical regularity deployed against chance, purpose pried with further leverage, moving earth when on the earth—decomposed granite, delinquent willows, human attributes given. Against stubborn silence, compacted molecules, dull ache of repeated conclusions. Ability to remind: kerosene, pine sap, antiquarian prepositions move narration shelf to shelf, down to sea bed, the other world absented from you. Returned with these scrapings: handful of sea bits, incompletion provoking their own pattern, skinny line upon which antiquity is run, tied off for now, residual tension communicated through, so double knot.

Crack open prior belief bicameral brain, unhusked, shimmy of halves clam-like in grey and white how taxonomy can account for parts' subparts, use of numeration in sectioned early modern treatise. Structure becomes us, attraction of phrasal units stepped into wet sand. His dog expects him to use the food metaphor again alluding to mysteries beyond quotidian but necessary examples. Ungainly clatter represents the quality and degree of unreliability, a canvas and wood aero plane coughs into operation, we are connected to our pilot's time scraping behind this year's calendar. Having made remnants evidence, elevated sand to legibility, conventions of this and that, over there, too.

*

A shock of seed corn so prosaic it takes on ancient aura (it's hard for me to see the children suffer). In fields we are separated by season from how abundance impressed tired people to more work as if correlates can give longevity to core principles. Dead-time, its inner eye's most meditative state: truth of plants dependent on what is conveyed through capillary structures, a traditional disputation transpires its green breath outward, a bloom of development giving foundation to natural heretics. When the story halts its approach at the linguistic border, what has been consummated by this lapping, lulling sound? Its big structure with a lot of props debates triumphant emptiness even here in this alternative, trial state. A thin coat: flaws of benign humanism?

*

A responsible self on the stand later re-constructs orders taken in The Hague. How moral goodness comes to resemble restraint in a crashing split-field of action. Hand to temple, cupped hand in back of stranger's head, a syntax naked as gravity? A visit to the *Pietá* to behold the sacred image—how might this exceed language?

*

Researchers portray optimal conditions, take count, death a reliable repetition framed in morality tale, temptation where artifice enters exceeding parameters of real life, lapel's jeweled insect. With cranes a city is "written" that is, on time, material, morphology of right angle, scissor truss, and narrow set of variables: proof by example, by weight-bearing chart. The point is to remove unknown, to reduce error, collapse, allow wings to operate by instrument panel if vision becomes disrupted. Burrowing animals build in excess, an economy of planned collapse, stoic requirement of over-work aesthetically incompatible with hyperkinetic moves, short runs, jerks. An individual becomes "individual" in a portrait—magnified departures from conventions of beauty, the long slide toward quotation. Has visual recognition a cultural import, angle-braced hall of mirrors?

Another way is flat, goes along minimal ground, and attracts the eye, along shoreline scalloped repetition on material that doesn't count. The portrait of that person is in the paint, no longer captured by looking beyond aperture's island, presence available on its surface, language's untranslatable sense. Folded between buildings—how they displace air—their rust, an idea in the spine. Insects, having eliminated experiment through accumulated understanding of frequencies felt by whisker, read for interpretive purposes, a relay of precise action, your one part passing to series, lengthening dissolution of particular to a run of pure monotone, white contrast, its fruit: index, a variation

*

When is the image a retort to technique? Narrative paired to display case covered forces involved: layers, time, great pressure, substrate ingredients. Hard not to imagine motive, plot toward development. Restless. Restless-ness, life below impact craters, water in wrong containers brought to impromptu shelters, hung like a scene, a moral of human worth—the mind goes, preceded by narrative trope. Conducted elsewhere, a pose or cry freighted with new economy of consequence or does the body inhabit classical grief based on musculature and limits? Increased snow and interference: the pavement, the presence of rhyme, case-hardened artifice presents itself, lays a claim to heart's natural beat. They lost us for now. How might distance collapse? Matched parts move from increased set to assembly? A bin of you's and them's snap into a whole product, another mentality, disk, disk-grinder to smooth difference to metal flake. A complete car-car by Wednesday, spokes gleaming.

Unbroken, youngest sister carries bottles freshly filled to decorate an ancient vase with effort at kinship? to repeat the oldest action as solemn repetition? Water runs, people run water, time runs. When the mechanism breaks, exposing metallic frailties, linguistic theory seems effete with its untouchable grandeur of disconnection, cultural illusion. Efferent, basics could trickle to dearth, its enlarged plans, rubble foundations.

*

Imitative, a string of vocables made for city traffic, a coat, a liturgy of walking with crowds, a sentence opens with familiar weight as if naming television examples of bathos can save portent from the problem of induction. A scholar's flight pattern was called in, the commercial pilot received approval, set off. To disappear behind the work fore-fronted work as an unbiased gift selflessly donated for common humanity. Cold vacant days. Briefly animals imagine other animals anterior to shocked exit from mental theatres onto quotidian snow, a mere stone under paw, wardrobe call, disarming reminder of typical truths. Our pride in instrumental falsity, averted faces, how infrequently we have to think in terms of evolutionary success.

*

Having captured the mind of another, set off beyond unlikely sea foam monument, anti-plinth. Dusty area boiling with small animals, their burrow holes: by one dirt, freshly turned, an entranced consciousness. To write so that years later you can't recall the diaristic particulars of that day, recapture only a sense, a fractured tooth touched again and again, too sharp, too irregular, to let consciousness pass in its ghostly hall-walk to "sleep" on the white bed beyond the small door frame, its time.

Left alone, waterfront skyline disrupted by cranes' praying mantis over reach, by cables' steady line, had promised to spark better ways to everything. Had we eaten of the fruit, knew nakedly we could not stand to read another? The resurrected form videotaped in the mind was not yet death, nor its subsequent chant of duration. The old neighborhood, winter wind perpetually whistling through walls, how some homes had a hopelessness even in youth. Having torn the membrane between one and many, the portrait takes part in tradition, representation of absent people. This week's new insect hatched after consistency of high temperatures that mean nothing.

*

from

involutia

Part of a rich tradition of poetry and commentary, *Secrets of the Blue Cliff Record* contains some of the most known and least known koans. Luce Irigaray and Gilles Deleuze have accidental meetings as "Luce" and "Gilles" at study.

Luce Studies the Blue Cliff Record, a little opera

Haven't I?

Haven't I said that?

Haven't I made enough?

So if she is restrained from images
        except through him, we have a problem
        of subjectivity
But her body could be other than his version
        A defensible space for
        creation of things
A name not closer to nature as a sensual flow
        but evocative exploration of sexual fusion
Accomplished by woman & man
        without dividing roles.
Does not adhere to grid, follows
        heat of the moment
Not clearly laid out or articulated.

        *

At high noon, there's no need to point east
        or define west anymore.
Yet conditions persist, how to take pulse of ailing
        or relieve pain?
        Did you walk all over with those
dirty shoes on?
            Turning your back
on interpretation as if literatures were
the size of a thumbnail
falling into type?

…A time that follows heat
of the moment, beyond particulars,
　　　　names, and distinctions.

　　　Giving oneself to be shaped
in a manner she cannot predict
　　　　To enhance the porous nature
of the body—moment to moment
　　　　Made an act mutual with time,
a membrane of pleasure
　　　　Pursuit of what cannot be represented,
but why the philosopher's task
　　　　of regenerating whole cultures?

　　　　　　　*

This is why closing and opening
　　　　are equally taught.
Perception joined to application
　　　(holding still)
　　　temporary is true: expert shows
　　　her moves to a weak opponent
　　　　　　　　　　Be sure not to glance aside
at new plants with weak roots.

As a condition that makes it
can break it: unrepresented yet constitutive.
Can read the texts for bias & subordination,
discover a new subject
lurking in the wings.
Not premised on lack, she unsettles
contemporary structures of language.
Without overlooking theatrical space-time,
its props & dialogs, steep recess into distance,
its splayed forefronting of intimacy or action,
she said, "specular economy."
To speak of thresholds & fluids,
shape of eroticism rather than scoping
detached parts, pliable
"landscapes."
So risking confusion, we must.

*

The philosopher, to say it in everyday terms, came to the edge
of the stagnant water of transcendence.

To cut through interpretations before the mirror
       loses its light.

The whole scene reveals your culture, its
       sound and form—an absorption in frolic.

without neglecting characteristic fluids
without neglecting characteristics of property
without neglecting characteristics
                                      that are tactile
        that are difficult to idealize
        that are difficult to make stable
        that are difficult to resist

Here, rubbings between two infinitely near
        neighbors
        stirrings between two infinitely near
        neighbors
        blendings between two infinitely near
        neighbors

There, a break between perceptible & intelligible,
        a break between mounting a scale of value,
        a break between "nature" put onto nature

                                    *

If you have eyes, look!

If you have hands, touch!

This is no more mystic…
than words *straight to the point*,
clear as pond water.

sensual forms through which perception
        manifests,
no over-emphasis on sight

there is a space between phallic gods &
  the rest of the world

she may cover & dwell in all things

  how closed is the word from everything?
how happy when both reflect, and so make the other?
  or not all, but a small, small angle.

     *

Without dwelling on anything, four gates.

Go on through, standing erect like
the free birds we are.

A flow, a percolation,
a favored edge.

       when he is forgetful of *she* who gave birth to him,
a protégé is born
       from a sea
       of becomings
is the "he" pronoun,
"I" prosthesis
       at false center of false pattern
linking events by corrosive illusion
       without exalted matter,
       we-they-you-she
             at passages

*

A monk shouts, then hits another
so radiant light is emitted
from bugs, dirt, and worms

"no guts" & "high opinion of himself"

slip, slip, slipped from the picture

       inherent properties
       (spliced with language

had we looked keenly
toward theatre conventions
              to penetrate Western thought
its geometries,
     overview, its slow dissolve?

what word describes a "*what* without properties
necessary for conventions with properties"?

             *

whiskers of an ant

one pound of feathers, weigh it yourself!

blinded by clichés, enter an *empty* valley.
     When will you ever get out?

Gilles Studies the Blue Cliff Record, a little opera

I have experienced the "arrival scene"
as if it were my own.

I have fallen-in-love as a cultural
trope with all its features.

I have perpetuated inequality without
awareness or disturbance of everyday life.

I have recognized backlit heroic
stances as objective reportage.

*

Making a gesture of fright: cane
        thrown down, a way
            of handling the snake.

Obliterate tracks, standing as a state.

Look at your feet as *expedient* means,
        look to the figure within a word
              as figurative, by rate.

        parts inside others, the way

we distinguish them from other things
presupposes stratified societies that select
        certain
        connections
        over
        others
What of other syntheses? connections?
        dynamic flows? fluid feelings?
        (propulsions that can also dissipate)

        *

Diamonds are tested with glass
        Zennists with a single word.

How are tests tested then?

The better grindstone
wears down dull edges.

Go where no one can spy,
        but how is everywhere made even more?

      double negation
      he is not that he is
      reactionary nomad

subjectivity as outcome   implications
      happens to fall
      from his own perspective
      to excessive birth of genre
and synthetic trope.

                *

I'm not a great teacher either
      I've already told you too much.

Is it something descended from heaven
      (a precious sword?)
Is it something that welled up from earth
      (an element that gives or takes?)

myriad forms & dimensions
      the little cup afloat
      raises a wave.

(Sources include: works by Irigaray, by Deleuze, *Secrets of the Blue Cliff Record* (Thomas Cleary, translator), and *Irigaray and Deleuze: Experiments in Visceral Philosophy* by Tasmin Lorraine).

Animated States

Uncertain on structure's relation anymore
to containment or plenum, an eligible

subject mounts with time making accrual
a force less set-like than a hard summons

of injustice defined in the immediacy of a crowd's cry.
Long, slow, subtle remedy washes over incompletion

even adding more fractured dispersal to old-time stories;
parsed by theme, comparativists roll out by rack,

the tree, its "up" side read as text, not agency
of circulation, a soul's voyage on tired road

uphill giving weight to mortal objects cast aside
conditioned by such context as two-fifths pain

makes the man to legalistic cohorts so rational
to administer and *fair*, as legible as waves,

though consider for a moment difficulties fraught
with decline and you have an explosive situation

on your hands, tilted track beyond switch-yards
and right-of-way conflagration fed by sparked

weeds, though ahead of myself here, analysis runs
from naturalized narrative and back until change

inhabits structure ghosting the screen moderates
claim they can bring to crisp clarity, adjustments,

moving furniture, re-seating the seated, who,
once again, managed to lose entrusted with it all

down to spent round establish optimism.

Midnight in Our Motivated

Right here, an alternate reading or despair our conditions?
Suggestion of foul play makes us experimental partners tentative

in keeping beat as nationalist pulse that races,
arranged in steps. But then coming down, erratic

words in mold and stale bread, informational or distilled
story, no unturned example, unpermitted dumping

altogether-now when most attacked historically—
At reading, our meter for conditioned signs now bypassed,

valid signature, worked valve, slick-faced
interference, rolled up welcome mats, suspicion—

now that's another story: hopped up percussionists
hum of air tankers on return circuit 'til it's out

emphasizing old taints and favors, impediments
liked for charting counterintuitive voting patterns

believers are no longer pulled inward to its great
or sundown, whichever comes first. A new science,

a sort of confusion using bad foot to drag good
as two ends reach across states' suspension.

Hadn't you hoped for a change adding fire,
telling-knots addressed to mind by hand, but the music

acquired measure runs its blood circuit, what's there
after midnight in our motivated glacial moraine. None.

No software adequate to discern delusion, an error
behind favoring the favored, never happens

yet how little we know of the world's composition
in just societies even in legislative form

or social constraint, those forces holding power of refusal
to natural domination, ill-gotten releases.

Products from agricultural regions compete for last:
feathers drop after double barrier, world becomes wide.

Irresistible volume to pattern desire, define equally
as mystify, knowing deferral works well—

boulder and drag-marks behind the car's embankment.
                The means already upon us completes
our education by vanishing, tools stuck with range:

limits embellish mortal compass with blurred sides, so true

Necessary Truths

after W. V. Quine

    1).

If little of our goings-on
go on
by necessity,
    then little need for a word like

necessarily.

It ain't prescriptively so.

People go on:
Went on, much went on by necessity.

    2).

If nearly all our goings-on
go on
by necessity,
    then little need for a word like

necessarily.

It goes without saying.

        3).

Passing events are sorted
                      not sorted

by features of necessity.

        Will it also make me sick?
(not necessarily)
      Surely he will miss me
      when I'm gone?
(necessarily, bound to)

        4).

When more sure than sure,
      no need for "surely."

If about to be shown a leopard,
      "surely it has spots"
           is predicted, so
out it comes
at leash-end

           governing the conditional sentence.

Pets

                         1.

The sacred icons: Jackie's gloves, auctioned
document, curated iris

      more sacred than these this spring…

from debased work conditions, we turn to love
      can my skin your skin
           touch
      without ideology of valentine
without spectacles
                of the kind our kin bear?

How I like our "mere appearances."

2.

"The individual who in the service of the spectacle is placed in stardom's spotlight is in fact the opposite of an individual … In entering the spectacle as a model to be identified with, he renounces all autonomy in order himself to identify with the general law of obedience to the course of things. … And Kennedy the orator survived himself, so to speak, and even delivered his own funeral oration, in the sense that Theodore Sorenson still wrote speeches for Kennedy's successor in the very style that had done so much to create the dead man's persona."

from Guy Debord's *Society of the Spectacle*

3.

Creating the dead's persona

(the absolute becomes historical)

as ever present power turns to close the door against winter
        and all our surroundings surround us
                in their contingencies

        gen: many one and one and one
              depend from
              penned from
    rendered pretty
    so pretty, we're blind
            but now eye sea
    general forms
    in particular
                stances,
    that's got his own

handle
in complement,
neck in advance

***

Spin animal tales horn
experienced chiffon, the red horse
      Mercury cut into lobes
and trivial decoration

hesitations

from

Goodbye Tissues

American Possessions

        far, black lung
                knot-spent, gas paltry

decimal, organelle, go?
    convey the stepped day
by horn blast, retinal
               hinder written or damned
"already"- town.

                *

de facto's unintentional hopped-theme

rationality's principle of difference
give over knowledge of singular thing

multiplication's individual
        demonstrael immunity
corpum, lump in the stomack
        sits there, of cause's relation,
elational load, paymaster of intelligible form
        quiddities, camber, the give in *it*,
how imaginary animal runs to type,
phoenix to trait
return's tonical home, old Kentucky or
        sweet's Chicago.

                *

after Lance Phillips

speech's speech
 amygdalae's portion *we* sounding—is peanut
wasn't converse hair, place am minimalist

That blowup click to size

Partner's trade one third.

*

rain's
satiation
of intermediaries,
down-splashing, minds, other forces fail…

Why subtlety's height runs sublime, ends
nourished, western painters, and doctrine.
These mountains' long neighbors, but
is despising earthly things how we teach?

This nations' enemies belong to war. Scripture
where the lowest go, toxic outflow beyond
fruitful bounty

who bindth water from this pool
distills life from poison, an order of sufficiency
to life
whose power.

*

Goodbye Tissues

                                        Goodbye tissues.

Purity (lens) contains one unit
        and two bottles of solution.

Common sight, however, is understood as neither including nor
excluding subtraction of defect since that would rule out the possibility
of understanding it as in a being which is sometimes beside existence.

Slim (jewel) case may be the case wherein
space saving abides. As a rewritable pack, you return
to what is there.

Diamond sutra of exempla: if what we directly write are alleged representations or copies of experiences we never see, from which we must then infer the experiences copied, we have no reason to think that the copies *are* copies of anything.

Yet there are no writings at all, only illusory mental states that compose minds.

A case of dianoia.

Dimensions of filter say "so long" for now.
Here, our basket holds short notes.

For example, *body* is defined as constituent of flavor and accent. However, because proper principles of accidents are not always manifest, sometimes we take the differences of accidents from their effects, such as dispersion or concentration produces differences of colour, insofar as there is an abundance or paucity of light, from which the different species of colour are caused.

Take it black. Amen.

Time, a sustained release, yet our incised tablet
won't last a day.
Can supplement-facts truly supplement
what is theoretical?

Is another doctrine necessary? But any doctrine must be of existing things, since there is no science of non-being. There are many supplements to the practice of series in literature, nature, mathematics, and theology.

All fiction is formed of language.

A thing should be repaired by the one who made it; one should reconcile oneself to all things.

Tents and watered gardens
near rivers.

Aquinas: *division textus*

                                                    Aquinas
two of three tractates where
we find *consolation*

                                        one
                    three   two

close analysis of the text
(division textus)

                            ┌─────────────┐
                            │ afterword   │
                            │ questions   │
                            └─────────────┘

The Exposition of Boethius' whether the human mind
On the Trinity   bodily eye
                            ourselves
                            through
                                it
                                    look ate man
                            as the his
                                to the illumination truth
                            blank sufficient in us, unable

                                            *

(various procedures, constraints, &
defacements of Boethius'   mind need mind
Consolation of Philosophy   truth does.
                                    stated "Not perception
                                       mind, lean, those learn,

Article 1: Does the human mind need   unless Teacher can eye
a new illumination of divine light for   as
knowledge of the truth?   by
                                                then
                                        light to be but labour

                                            *

light to be but labour
        twofold second
        the first
        light for
        of God

it is— one, does
knowledge of— first question
light in   it seems
2 Corinthians   '… think anything …'
Therefore, the   illustrated anew

it is   it on
to those,   learn from
say in   thirty point three
is illumined as the
intelligible things
eye can the material
it, is, acts are
for their   three-are

          *

                            third in alternates

so, therefore we   within us principles
we must be   truth in order
operation of the   human mind is

light than the   of lower sensible
have forms which   principles of natural
cannot bring off   the stars on

increases them, therefore   neither does the
as it were   human mind to
light namely the   supervenes the same

causes are ordered
and not *per*

first cause

                        *

after Hölderlin

Article 3: Is God the first thing
known by the mind?

      Against thought held by
dreaming snakes
      we judge what we know
as first-light necessary to sight, so
we might have *things* in light.
      First, the sky swivels from
a pinhole held to cathedral spires
      where rain falls on intelligible
things, perception a still life
from which human perception
is stenciled—second to
eclipsed presence.

Why might planed wood
show creation extracted from
raw scenes, set primacy?

      But no, first or last, our boat
let to cradle-rock on perceptible waves
—how we live, each after sight of the face.

*

Further Articles

Article 4: Is the human mind sufficient
of itself to reach knowledge of the
divine Trinity?

"mode, species, order"

Funny, how we can see
a creature and not know
what it is. In the sky and forests and
 seas and theology.

Stars magnify everything.

The creator and its mind: two.

We trace to makers, a word.

Sharing gives us joy.

Fragments proceed from whole.

We might think of what precedes
inequality as prior equality.

Three is perfect.

Mode
species
order.

*

On the contrary:

three=one

satisfied animals are solitary

three days of sacrifice

looked to unknown effect

when a word doesn't link the two

not all arguments are exhausted here

we note distinctive circles

even if distinctions are taken away,
      joy remains

little bodies, celestial bodies

meaning of equality; causes of plurality

a number as a form of completion

many can be *one* here

known in its relations to other things

        *

On Goodness in General

Article 1: Do good and being differ in reality?

        The striped green awning of dollar stores.

        Parrots' complaint this morning.

        China said to buy up their daily fare.

        No correspondence to autobiography.

        Mexico begins maybe three hours from here.

                *

        Most made things, of artifice.

        Things salted with a sense of time
        that is not metaphysical.

        Striped, serial items, re-prints I couldn't
              manage to imply, or was implying.

                *

*

With a damaged fuselage, another
show of approbation.

*

Article 3: Is every being good?

added, plankton, planksheer
 contracted skin, fell-kin

resuscitate, hauberk, throw?

 relay arrow's deck
by sawbuck, Esquimaux
 virtue, a drift or prime
flaw-trench, mere nurture.

*

       near, scenes brachiate
prefrontal's Flemish peasant—arm
wasn't flipper, body

protected unpalatable's drop
lay between
rounds' determined range—

                 *

explanatory weight: cephalic
lobe in colony, canopy.

       *

(Portions of the preceding segments titled "Goodbye Tissues" through "On Goodness in General" derive from various sources including Thomas Aquinas' *Summa Theologiae* in a range from slightly doctored forms of citation to forms of severe disintegration.)

Four

        part martyr
where linger came

    they say   … clemency of oaks
as if there were

    not possible to lever words
with more

    yet what we do, marled
thing loves its weight

"…to assert a normal hum
until, that is, the
great big cork tag
of the jury's verdict
rows of boxes
watching many famous figures"

from *Eternal Sections* by Tom Raworth

1.

By section, we're bound to realism,
assures us light necessary, breath may
lead to project and provisional set,
outsized authorial negations or
umbrage at lack of indictment, build is
by state. Here, erased ledger-reference,
our myth with metonymy: folding lamp,
the swerve in pollen's Brownian descent
"bee" applied for, procedural text can
not without blueprint, refined intention,
précis: its honey setting. And today
its copied *build*, body, array marked
more shutters and paralysis echo
toward parity, fourteen lines, more or less.

2.

Render a proof, engulf the war or
use of images (presence) to suggest
residue and residual salt, air-
open as the times require—thus people,
one burning issue to rally around.
On the Potomac persists a marble
national axiom at a hill's height,
theological view of pollution,
evaporation of memory. Our
port egress vigorously marked off or
submit to *nothing*, select against "their"
irrational fear. Deliberately
duet in artistic farce derived from
exploitive *intelligence* as it's called.

3.

They see rows of Renaissance plays. Second
projected onto spring rains, where poor food
smells provide a third stage, make dust and heat
"de-anchored from place"; never mind we can.
Voices fill the theatre: their faces shine.
This is not at the farthest remove from
a laugh nor from Ezekiel's prophesy
but tilted outward, our non-celestial plane.
Of three stages: the bed and pillows are
not had at the train station, electric
sensations abstracted to principles—
go sense the same eternal smell anytime.
An unethical practice to save lives?
Our vanishing point recession:
                                        state house to tiny dot.

4.

A dragon assembles a bride-machine.
Middle-period know-how slides to form,
loose study to specialty amplified
at first hint of dragon. Our knight opened
an explanatory parenthesis.
Open parentheses create suspense
that Hegelian dialectics won't
satisfy. A preface may signal troop
deployment, yet the most quotable are
withdrawals from Tikrit that offer three or
more branching paths, a crystalline organ.
Too often, travelers use trees when they
enter a clearing. The knight replicates
item, meaning turned a hazard ground.

10.

The speech-writer changes position. Noted
for a prompting "On evil," a moral
term helped the president gain favor. Boiled
the syrup until, against the wooden
spoon, a viscous wave showed transformation
to cold solid. The many vanishings
of the subject. Yet, footprints of a "been,"
or a "was," photographed here, a lab slide,
tissue sample. The sonnet's rhythm makes
our effigy burn bright. The "go-away"
chant of bright vultures double-click with "here
you are," "there you go." Corpuscle ending
to a secondary nerve. Vegas, called
back, so one promise made good on right here.

11.

Not all hypotheses are utopian
as well as logical. Nation within
reservation. General Electric
state, their nuclear waste. How Argonauts
sometimes are the expense of the mother's:
nine plus nine plus one years I've lived right here.
Just blank out lines, reinscribe time so we're
a proposed case that could be disastrous.
This nation exercised rights, made laws as
their herd of blind deer in western New York
held a hard position against the banned
life. "I" am leaving for another place.
Language is lastly forgotten. Sonnets
now pose: what brave new world is for sale now?

Coda

after Celan

Good-bye.
Good-bye, Good-bye.
Marked by place,
star-set, word—
go to rest, our result.

Go to rest, our result.

Was, was
truth. How did we
get over—get over
with these words?

Speckled,
Speckled and leonine. Blade-
shaped sort –wort, constellate,
shallow-rooted

it did not take more than
we had, it made a show of
itself, a show
raised us up

       it repaired
the skin of our place
and figured water,

figured
figured water—then

a bird, a training bird
swung from a string

rocks a shadow uphill,
a shadow uphill,
no shadow
for the learned came in.

      *

made, made
up,

We wanted to be taken in,
to take in.
Our natural parts
were always there,
and it obliged.

Obliged us, obliged
our fabric, and cleared
each cell, then

        no film to cover
those fixed in place, would pond.

Cover and fixed in place

Let in, let on
that portion, fabric
cut to clothe.

Island and capital
made over.

      *

from

Depleted Burden Down

Procuratio

How is it that the long draw-down from a set of commonplaces whether first or second, here or elsewhere, an array of parts or the arrangement itself, the divide between meaningful and deviant became irreconcilable in scope and intent to rhetorical devices now useful to resisters? To be a limit case, one citizen went in for the panel-style tattoo as if artistic tradition woke from a somnambulant press of time, changed horse by post, then changed back as the horse of translation.

Irony and introspective sketches, erotic and religious themes: the color of justice, one could argue, grounded simple conditions.

Here are letters and numbers. No grand act to follow with one less grand. No spooky sense of inheritors that never cancels out scratchy and hiss-perforated source of influence in a Freudian comedy of repression undone. To be trapped in the logic of representation disallows what we are here about: minor islands, these desires. A cough or secondary rash—not theme of entropic unwinding here.

But this folding knife, this toad-stabber or father-killer was distributed to all veterans of World War II in bivouacs and colleges, out on the road, and in jars. Truths of that time & place—force of thought, forced to thought. Could echo be distinguished from direct quotation, and further, could that distinction save authorship, originality, things our nationals are good at? Suspense in how the prince of Denmark is revised by the master, yet hasn't the master written our very world? Let us read on and see.

In the socialist ideal, theory met practice, and some of us went to visit varying post-revolutionary moments. In Havana, I was asked why Buffalo poets are not the same as the New York school poets: "Buffalo is in New York, right?"

Of self-emptying systems: nihilism. How can "yes" displace "no"? Sunyata replete.

But a substitution theory: the word for the thing, the thing for the other thing, has a "universal" appeal. It's money. And little in the way of theorizing can interrupt its commerce, its erotic appeal. This rainy heartbreak, that dime-store by the ear of the mob, face out loud. Keep ocarina far from selvage: blew, then method and mathematical certainty. Haul and scrape good Word for importation to godhead, poached and re-set, spring mechanisms and all. Executed by market track, human capital, finance group, our prize, seminar on human entourage if you have the software, foundlings' Houdini, erased land, term professor, robot message. Hard to see the go-between we are.

Mild lamb of the hour where emphasis fell on the value of conceptual appeal, how a tender cube might carry allusion, owing formula to flow … so, matters change, a pagan stance an incorporeal narrator takes, not to conflate that state with omnivorous childhood wilds, its youth

$$\diagup \qquad \diagdown$$
     formation   dissipation

There installed: a quantity of prose, citations, stamps (brief, dactylic and diminished spondees), inscriptions, images (daring and insipid). Thus is one very different from the protagonist about whom you read? A peasant habitus—read with cynic pleasure on Horacian rustic scenes, one Southern winter where dispositions come to be.

Tomcat calls
porous, a bear follows, warm yourself in his hut briefly, same movie
dream-sequence in that work of early days: who sits at the table but
hippogriffs & lion-headed men, goat-bearded giraffes, electronic
peddlers into the bargain taking fifty for two, a common collection &
book in bed looked into causes, interpretations, synthetic applications
and skipped to the lou my darlin'   to your
maker address this conflict: *I* feel faint
Here, alone, our nebulous journey is brief. Born a people, and to die for
that is sad.

So an image version of language might take up maize that is genetically modified, alienation at home and at work better than a threat of offensive procedures begun with tanks. Whether the ability to express mental images with which "we" may empathize such as "their" plight, wages, and shortages that occur on the Cartesian flat screen that is mind or to purvey a set of resemblances between Lockean ideas and things is not what provokes us to step toward the podium and begin a primary language game.

Before people realized the effect of windblown pollen no fighting broke out, and women, for the first time, faced a collection of flaked-stone implements that spoke in the manner of contemporary linguists of propositional attitudes—thought, beliefs, intentions. Depressed, our favorite satirical cartoon understood the off-flow, seepage, and downstream effects, the consequences of a nation's independence, free elections forcibly held between factions that unlike Newtonian gravity were subject to international monetary policy, and so came into fields no matter fenced areas, signs.

But put off principled involvement is not our only shot at rights, so much derived from social practice, so much went without funded scientific determinations too long against unregulated kinds of open pit extraction, conventions that govern what speakers mean, getting you to believe and conceive.

Could have saved on furnishings, saved from outside's perimeter, cruel history. Of the types of manslaughter, where the hands are macular's vault of semiprecious numeration, grain-count's other body yoked to concurrence, place. How else a post-slavery economy made to re-make pulverized flour, consensus' loan, pork count's back ranked cuts by examiner, packaged on business tables, smoked out and vacated—old melody's purveyor, disfigured swamp child, fell sway of influence, national effort.

Early Soviet Cinema

— Vertov poems —

…common period by hangar.
How many times the clock has no purpose?
                              In its relation to other

clocks, self-similar row, city by city, exemplar
of un-Bergsonian time; position
a rapprochement between orthodoxy and travelers.

A means to immobilize duration,
claim to make particle, heritage that swell
of memory uncovered by tissue, gesture.

A doomed organism with a movie camera,
plow by rhyme, subtracted-material groove,
the *why* in why our icons mourn, had once.

— Vertov poems —

Pokes the air
with his finger
      Trotsky

warrantless
surveillance
passed

on one
side

America
tumbled
on other

turned sideways

neckties
of varied colors
            intertitle

     tumbled
on other side

turned

neckties
of varied colors

pokes the air
      Trotsky
            intertitle

warrantless
surveillance
passed house

on one
side

America
        turned sideways

a sign
of varied colors

with his finger
        Trotsky

tumbled
        turned sideways

on other side
        surveillance

America
turned neckties

with his finger
on one
side

Trotsky tumbled
America

of varied colors
on other   intertitle

turned warrantless
        on one

surveillance
neckties poke the air

America tumbled
sideways

of varied color
Trotsky

warrantless house
on other

Translation, the bass accompaniment

1.

The word. Period. Periodization, as a sequential process.

The province of the right point, more exact than dotted points.

This argot like punching adventurers of film, ethnology.

Derived points from Latin, or a minimal extension of "thing".

There are painters who before they paint go across,
        anticipate seeing images across discrimination.

They leave white to the image; they don't go there.

Like a baby's head, they exit pugnacious lines of continuity.

They say the point of making progress converts the line.

But the line, it has not made progress.

Nor has the image.

To be an image is to play at continuity.

To play at statehood.

Absolute progress along a line is to close & make an idea
        found wanting: *ideation, figuration*.

To be the bird you have in your head? Painters have no heads.

2.

Three questions on where you place yourself
before you were consumed by life.

We have necessities in the interior city and libraries enough.

The province is a mode of seeing.

We have readings, seasonal winds, prejudicial locals.

I travel to the capital frequently—each year or every two years.

The alternative for the older generation is not ours.

My contacts have been more spacious & our dialog stimulating.

"Heat dilates corpses."

Many from my group have dispersed to France, Spain, Venezuela.
    I came to Mexico in the middle of the intellectual ferment.

The relations between art & life, for me, are impossible to negate.

Verbal material is a dialog with destiny.

Personally I prefer a life distant from literary circles where disputes
    and penalties characterize the place once separated from the
    noise of conciliation.

If something results in a poem—well, that is a miracle.

There is not a formula to repeat it.

Arrival

one hundred cigarettes, a daily commentary,
        chip, or cache of favor
        our guard might

make life bearable, swamp of pointless stops
        air not properly sealed
        the phone is not free

churned up mud, mudflat smell, dogs,
        aged-horn, clavé of train-track
        the poet said, inspired what degree

matter-parsed is matter, dull lump
        whether corkscrewed lathe-shavings
        or razor thin gaseous film

resumed offensive without warning, foam
        of nostalgic memories post-date
        how it felt, nitrate remainder

post-rain, chalk flats at a distance, improbably
        powdery close-up, descriptors
        built for containers, centennial parade.

Another interview

Investigate the truth of your time, the work of sputniks.

Let's be precise, no analog, no wooden sanctified tradition.

Human expression in fibers will result in predictable fabrics, so where are examples of the *ignorance-doctrine*?

Mostly, poetry is against having results.

During the last quarter of a century, poetry in this country differs in who has the bad taste to mention capitalism or not.

Half the people worry about where the poetry of our country is going; the other half worry about the status of their dialog with reality.

I agree: to write is to inscribe the world.

There are many realists. So their polemic, "realism," is a bit ingenuous. To pretend to be a photograph is not to accept poetry as the inverse proportion to its informative content—like our times of disinformation, we sit through such at school or how the mass media enters our heads—but the use of certain artifice provokes an illusion of reality.

It follows in what is tactile; its taste and smell are going to be unified and incomparable.

All our good current writers are reticent to be a party or school.

As an alley, "aesthetic" is a poor insult as are political pamphlets which never compare strongly nor become major.

I'm not interested in knowledge about knowledge, or art about art—they are all a trap.

Who needs a trap when we have a state of no functioning signs, violence, exploitation, and alienation?

There is no entertainment industry without a poetry of indignation.

We believe in a parallel universe to Language, yet plunge right into the medium of language.

It is not more important for your listener, this reflexive scene.

Apotropaic Shuffle

Of disagreements on the history and function of the apostrophe, some sources say it's used for missing letters or had a start as a printer's mark to indicate omission, but more interesting is the claim the "cumbersome name for an awkward mark" is rooted in the Greek phrase to "turn away" from the audience when addressing another person.

Still others show mere possession complicated by, perhaps, eight genitive cases. Here we've used it: space constraints in newspapers, compressed words in rap lyric, text message, advertising. Typically seen and not heard, these marks attempt to dispel confusion. Not having exhausted *possession* as cultural insertion of devil into the dance or fervor into rhetoric, punishment into excess, message into the medium, we go on.

Some see the result of homophonic confusion (there's and theirs or it's and its) leading to the death of apostrophe as a required mark in standard English. With time, companies dropped the mark in advertising and street signs. The US Board on Geographic Names has done the same. How to represent speech in written form…

In the strict sense, without importation of non-literal reference, no sleight of hand, no switcheroo of word for other word, or thing for other thing, but straight-up, no chaser.

So, adhere, outside the walls of some Palestine our finite lamp on small motorcycle, paper with rain forecast, vague smell, promulgation of humility all serve to position last properties, poured oil, extracted. We lose all power; nothing to do in shadows. Moving shock, odd frontier in crude letter, that liturgical authority—the demos dead so how advance? what massed weight above this column?

John Langshaw Austin's "performative utterances" occur when a person is *doing* something rather than *saying* something, and he gives examples: witnessed oath, an apology, ceremonial naming or conferring, waging a bet verbally, all so the saying is the doing. The circumstance must exist—one cannot swear an oath alone in the bathtub, conventions for giving a witnessed oath must exist and be accepted, he writes. That efficient cause: weight, heat, purpose are not mentioned.

"Infelicities," Austin writes, include inappropriate circumstances or insincerity, or both, or misuse of performative utterance by a political insurrectionary or wax in your ears, or use in a play, joke, or poem… Neither radical nor poet, he discusses the performance of [I] "promise that…" but somehow he misses that we report a promise made by a president years back that was both unfulfilled and contingent on the public's short-term memory.

Question now defunct: mind and its location, duration of mind with onset of neuro-finding, and academic philosophy gets re-structured. The Las Vegas mentalist learned there are predictable ways people think from his years as a repair and maintenance man in a Vegas mental hospital. He could predict the number anyone might select from a range of numbers. Each time he dazzled with his ability to predict selections made by volunteers in his night club audience.

He knows, he said in his radio interview, the patterns of human "evolved" brain function, reads them like a book.

If Quine thinks sensory stimuli is all we have "to go on" in arriving at our knowledge of the world, it seems a mentalist could give us the predictable pattern our brains make of those stimuli.

Why the capacity (or, at least, evidence) for self-correction is seen as a feature of artificial intelligence, science as a field, balance in walking.

X lives on the smooth, frictionless plane of scientific observation.

Our innate sequences. Such as they are.

The big question is how we the audience can be so compellingly entertained by the feats of the mentalist.

The trick of self-similar growth expressed in systemic theory, how the cool contractions coalesce; hulks and wrecks of old tankers beached for parts, discontinuous topography certainly re-labels smooth welds *junk* and collective identification *ontology of dead ports* sludge-filled locks. Anticipating serial production: cast plaque, necklace panel, harness ornament, jury of peers, the do-right notion of predicate to truth function. It's about the world, the language we use, proxy function. Will that bit of light characteristic of time stand in for theft around us?

from

Saccade Patterns

Keep, a Melodrama

W. V. Quine: "To be is to be the value of a variable."

Threadwaste

Everyone went there to be seen by someone.

Send six, or five, of your best.

Evening as a differential equation
        from here, barred in triple reveal,
loose change blocked from view.

The ripped out, free matter roughly torn
from tripods of western perspective, now
        only somewhat recognizable
lumped here, more garbage than sourcebook.

That some came from rolls…
fell a manufacturer's sortage plan—
        down, deft, voter-less. That impression
so negligently made recurs at what noise level?
Bent back, thin straw paper soggy
with it, grid to equidistance one from one another
so no conversation, disgruntled sub-vocalizing
makes jointure of pain, rip-off by degree
        saccade coverage where mitigation enters late.

As part of habitat gotten up to resemble savannahs

star-like
concerning a formal system, try to dance

meager drizzle in cement channel

no longer permitted to independent
observation: plaque, umbrellas, rote memorization

airplane overhead
headache from excess
light, too bright

operators yet improvability
marshals much evidence to illustrate arbitrary claims
carried out with finitary methods

others
others have forearm across brow
light, too bright
food, untouched

Opercula, fall off as they open

Poincaré: "I protest above all against the use of an infinite quantity as a *completed* one, which in mathematics is never allowed."

                 Strange combinations, some Justinian
plus Neptune, civil claim for addition, apse for infinite set,
mathematician in his prohibition against completion
that here is merely one of four mythic phases of the earth. It came out from
the insides of Mediterranean life, its gizzard a straw heap
vaguely donkey temperature, practice of rennet mostly local,
something not on paper, not a king-like god, so the other eye
exceeds the start
come round again swimming here, clothes weighted with water, from eye
a tiger-tined metal sinks, that is
negative from oarlocks' drip, undulate sheen of cathedral lights
recursive for now.

B: To claim abstract thought for apes? Primatologists have been burned too often.

A: What about math? With two hands, base 10 seems a bodily extension. How hard could that be?

how much computation possible without language?

eucalyptus caps (one-to-one correspondence, derive
            symbol for word-logic, other items
                for relations, i.e., if…, then…)

groundskeeper rakes them away

                                        past addition
how to conceive of multiplication, observation of moon
in relation to solstice observation of aligned bar of sun,
sets of days → months → years

psychology of nuclear primate family imposed
          misrepresents set as complete

projection of eucalyptus caps
—what is "between" each one?
—how can infinite amount be in relation
                                to itself?
—why the ongoing puzzle of how 0, 1, 2
have unique properties?

So, start with something simple, base 10, what if one eu-cap for 10 digits,
then 10 eu-caps now represent 100…

              *

is the point to compress large quantities
into small items, so then, several small
items can be manipulated more handily,
yet the full result can be expressed
when called upon to all place values

eucalyptus caps fall here
(or call them eucalyptus pips,
or gumnuts in Sydney?)
made small piles, made rows,
made outlines of circle, barred zone
filled in circle, barred zone with same

man in green work shirt, rake,
        barrel on wheels

provide a solution
to the general problem reduced
                  to special case

it seemed I had ignored protocol
for greeting others, dropped
handful of eucalyptus cap

                imagine:
a long tape of caps, from here,
along the length of habitat, down
the drainage gully then up to visitor
areas and beyond to parked cars, highway

and on, and on

and now imagine another set of same

what is the relation of the one to the other?

On seasonal change—

day-flies
feel it, visitors
their glandular smell

*

supposed to do my thing up here
            instead
I'll frame a question for them:

Could we think of variable extinction?

*

                    consequently
No more birth of veal)

how will thought halt,
where's a single groan

installed?

:Is it good to live so caged to name each variation of eucalyptus tree, of quantity and set, members of our band, sky, bars, man in green work shirt, visitors, dirt & sand, meager food not meant for migrants, scraps of music, stretched limbs never brought to momentum nor bath of air passed through at a run?

push themselves forward
        over there, over there

                *

      raid
      another raid

      sex & grooming
      more grooming

                *

not endogenous
        members' offspring

                              what, even with your ten thousand lives
wind, a trickster figure, rips leaf and paper litter along wall

one watches, waits
one sees
one frames

a plan in time, a fold
kept, a keeper, too:
here is my cricket, kept back in tree hole with array of sticks
        spaces set too narrow
        to come through
it chirps
just past barred light

                        birds fly toward the carousel & coach house as it warms
not toward keeper's hut and storage like when it cools

                    more sun
                    sour taste in food, hyper-feeling
                    edgy
monitors strapped here & there. I'm an experiment.

exertion, so if force and instrumentation
       make for my sovereigns
as in turn my cricket is for me

how is mind barred by them, in short
       does it participate? Can conscious sense of self

become king & queen of its own cerebrations
       ever social,
          an inter-speciation

*

hard not to see
visitors at railing—one big guy
lords it over others, or how that small
mean girl keeps her brother in check

       their gestures, squaring off,
          deflect, grovel—that woman who
makes her space small
in group of men

Pant-laughing
pant-laughing from the exercise yard
I will help group gather and peel food later.

*

What should I name the cricket?

:This is not a cricket
:Ignore the chirp
:The great zoo escape from within
:Steal this cricket
:Being plus-one if sound counts
:See, a primate can have a pet
:Won't last long
:Looks like last year's
:Knows my every mood
:Hear me? You never listen!
:A leaping orthopterous insect, male
:The kind we make cages for
:A bug beyond compare
:Potshot at evening
:Falls silent at death
:Wants sex mostly
:Incapable of abstract thought
:Passes genetic material without trace of poetic sequence
:A guy in black suit, ultra-nude
:Leaves no trace

man in green work shirt
        barrel on wheels, rake

two attendants in lab coats:
        wake up from black-black time
        dressing on left arm

They decide.
Or decision itself: is government a game?

A set of rules they use
derives from another more axiomatic set—their acts
hint at how they think, constitute
ethical treatment, denial of favor, even application or
higher purpose for pain right now, my swollen arm,
yesterday's induced sleep, drawn blood, monitors

an electrode extraneous to my original set?
        my mutable electric firings…

School for Perisarcous Considerations

Turned fully down, a new socket, felt farm: what is
felt for lint, language for an existential quantifier,
        elevated stanchions for sacrifice. Such

was industrial revolution rooted
in nomadism, rock-perch, and coal fire; such

was postmodernism rooted
in shift-pattern, delivery failure, and gladiatorial spiff; such

was modernism rooted
in drafting conventions, vertical reprise, and dirty dreams; such

was romanticism rooted
in answers to being called, floral swords, and machine-free cloth.

heavy rain, all sent inside

loud, loud
        Will
we fall out
of our shadows?

        Will the ending then
hesitate a bit
right through here? Your puddle.

                                        Lab again, what to see?
same arrangement—each grid in packing crate
three to one side
four to the other
                              openings
hand-holds, two

      :But then you see it's not about inventory, *Principia*, or any sort of complete directory with items and variant relations,

      it's how to represent generative proximities and iterative engines that jump tracks to move onto irregular landscapes.

press on

earn my keep

REM sleep:

I'm running at full extension of my arms and legs.

There seems to be a purpose.

Upon arriving to a clearing, startled birds fly upward.

Their formation tells me, right away, there are 240.

As soon as I grasp this formula, the birds are gone.

Somehow I began to fall.

Falling in what seemed infinitely slow time, an electric charge circulated at top speed around my head three times.

I'm aware of a burnt smell then woke here strapped to the gurney.

A lab attendant leaned over to look into my eyes.

How, the means

after Bill Viola's video installation entitled *Fall into Paradise* from his larger work *LOVE/DEATH: The Tristan Project* that was invited by the Paris National Opera for its production of Wagner's *Tristan und Isolde* (1865)

       I apply
       so you

                      how
underneath, what does this say
what does this want to say about want

you see
blouse opening

I see you see

yet thrum
black duet

      how
re-mastered
chanson, arteries

rapid climb
your nonvocable

on the plain

expand evenly

how with us common air
pierced the sea

      close the lid
light skirmishes there

rib-pattern
off and on

(who)
when you rode
to see
where I am

you found a copy
you thought would work

asunder, that city
ordinary message

       taken
on the plain, evenly
page screened there

       how is where,
our chorus has means
to mean

       pariah, it comes down
where do you go?

   named in the meeting room
        violence: being a topic

marked

our island, meek
can we paddle there

read a play?

        open to come,
comes back
your look
more and more
our separateness
in privacy
seen already
I empty
slip
your being over
me
your being there, here
make susceptible
how we
sequence

not saying so
there, here

                        how priests
keep us from being
gods, their formula

holy bodies, said,
know an ancient knowing

somatic inscription
marked here
            on him
            on me

for mind, said,
pleasure left
pungent word
(re-staged here)

                        how
                    preside over
end of it
end it here

potion, poison
chance, plan
tremble to bring it within

freed result, pairing:
his shelter, my cut

put on, put in

surface we crave
surface we lean in toward

what proof requires
what torment for inconsequential
words, but of three:

just thrown down
erected edifice
cloud-envelope

night over too soon
regained his pants, shirt, etc.

said, hasty
breathing breath

he wades into
a great internal design
soon to structure his world

I enfold.

Not a fall, at first,
how interpret?

release, second
we are released,
fall, fallen
come to

       (breathe)
scatter pieces

how they come to contain

                              war continued
despite our sanctuary
if I listened

inside I would hesitate
                                        hear
the world sound
authoritative—

shot sub-surface

        highways out
          to desert
proving grounds

movement toward
an uncovered origin,
outlandish control

Why are we here
where it's hot?

where, a site index

With hand on joystick

how Synthetic Vision technologies train pilots
how technologies adjust pictorial format and focus
how virtual reality helps re-train severely injured military personnel
how the use of GPS and Intertial Reference Systems solve navigation
    problems
how we are no longer flying blind
how 3D technologies with conventional perspective give pilots an "intuitive"
    feel for their flying environments
how the new boresight symbol (- V -) is in the center, and the horizon line
    shows pitch
how the Tunnel in the Sky is a conceptualization of flight paths depicted
    by visionsystems
how Enhanced Vision uses near-infrared cameras and millimeter wave
    radar in limited visibility environments
how head-up display (HUD) with predicted impact point (PIP) helps
    pilots make accurate hits with ballistic projectiles
how a glowing red dot appears over the weapon's impact point regardless
    of the shooter's eye position
how saccades help rods and cones refresh an image read by the brain, create
    continuity
how synthetic vision is used for Remotely Piloted Vehicles (RPVs) with
    control signals up-linked and aircraft telemetry down-
    linked to remote cockpit displays
how Synthetic Vision systems could have prevented the crash of American
    Airlines Flight 965 in 1995
how helmet mounted displays (HMD) move with the user's head relative
    to the airframe
how new experiments attempt HUD systems that project information on
    the inside of swimmer's goggles
how new experiments attempt HUD systems that project information
    onto the wearer's retina with a low-powered laser
how HUD designers consider that a person's eyes are at two different
    points and seek to prevent a person from re-focusing

between display and outside world
how designers attempt to accurately map display onto what the pilot sees
how altitude and speed are your friend when trying to deal with "unexpected events."

Weak as a directive, no

Weak as a directive, no vivid allegory
of bones-to-resurrection, thimblomachy, but
toy-cute: is the miniature an after-effect where the mechanism
might be a vast amount of text, say Leviticus
or Kama Sutra, inscribed on a caraway seed so
you need magnifying apparatus to read
ligature of plants, priests, and positions per seed surface?

Ekphrastic-generated streets held fancies and delights in line,
as well as slums and mufti despair, vying for dominance:
what group is more exclusive?
        Is it a pitchfork or a metonymic framework,
but no, it's the old *City of Quartz* story after all, the West
built by developers, disbelievers in public space,
who work their predatory boredom, a dynastic speed-up

in relation to populace. The hypothetical city each carries,
well-lit space, etc. in thrice-viewed movie, embrace of
gods fresh from Wardrobe whose grey buildings and
crowded sidewalks out-lurid our own origins, our own
sense of nothingness, so scan for departures from first
plan as if Cenozoic weight could shift us from paucity
of settlement, dented tin globe, Celestine rot not about
aerialists in crenellated domes or chimps in space, our
proxies might not latch shut helmet and deluxe harness,
might not take it anymore.

Lamb Notes

body, scale
        floor, covert
critique of full scale presentation

commonwealth
held high baby doll
head grafted to crow

slime strings
"Dirt of Tomorrow:
Agnes Dei"

sheep Catholic
icon, Zurbarán perfection of sacrifice

                *

lamp, perfection
lamb, order

dirt experiments, less
controlled, more tactile

tropism, gallery opening
and milling machine

Styrofoam angel head
Greco Roman

intricate delicate
lines onto repeated black tiles

*

album
in platinum vessel

deep visual connection
between idea & music

excess
               OR
attraction repulsion
to ordinary objects' design

lamp classic lines
       subtraction

lard, flesh & meat
   milking stool

attach where fat permits

                    *

broken bubble floor
                pattern

fleshless
        Caucasian skin
        see veins beneath

design & scent

booth of perfumer

100 year old lumber
from burned building—
analyze the scent
& we'll design around
that

                *

three parts for chopping block
symmetrical paired
                handles
voluptuous, but now a recession

*

These pages were derived from a talk entitled "Dirt of Tomorrow: Agnes Dei" given at SCI-Arc, Los Angeles March 17, 2010 by Zoe Coombes and David Boira on work at their design studio, Commonwealth in Brooklyn.

Biographical Note

Deborah Meadows grew up in Buffalo, NY, in a working class family, graduated from SUNY, Buffalo in Philosophy and English, then moved West. She lives in the Arts District/Little Tokyo section of Los Angeles with her husband Howard Stover. Meadows teaches in the Liberal Studies department at California State Polytechnic University, Pomona where she has been a faculty member since 1989. Her Electronic Poetry Center author page is located: http://epc.buffalo.edu/authors/meadows/

CPSIA information can be obtained at www.ICGtesting.com
Printed in the USA
BVOW011544130213

313181BV00002B/5/P